Unlocking the Public Realm: An All-Inclusive Handbook of Nevada's Notarial Procedures

Kristi J.Collins

Copyright :

About the author

Kristi has delivered a far reaching guide intended to give legitimate experts in the Silver State with the devices they should find true success in their professions.

With a solid energy for accuracy, delicate taking care of, and maintaining the best expectations of unwavering quality in notarial strategies, Kristi consolidates exceptional fitness with down to earth grasping in her composition.

Kristi J. Collins is perceived for her capacity to distil intricate, substantial ideas into compact, convincing language, in this manner empowering notary public of all experience levels to get to the handbook. Her objective isn't just to edify yet additionally to spellbind perusers, empowering them to precisely and easily investigate the subtleties of notarial strategy.

By perusing "Unlocking the Public Realm," Kristi welcomes perusers to go on an excursion of development, unwinding the mysteries of Nevada's notarial strategies and succeeding in notarial techniques. You can rely on Kristi to be your reliable and keen tutor while you seek after your notarial objectives and hoist your expert practice higher than ever.

Introduction

Once, Sarah had moved to Nevada to start her own business. As she adjusted to her new life, she discovered that the state had numerous odd laws and ordinances, including specific requirements for notaries. Sarah realized she would have to become a notary public in order to properly execute important business documents. She did, however, find navigating the notarial requirements and procedures difficult and confusing.

Sarah wished she had a comprehensive guide to help her grasp the subtleties of Nevada notarial practices because she felt overwhelmed and unsatisfied. Her wish was fortunately granted by "Unlocking the Public Realm: An All-Inclusive Handbook of Nevada's Notarial Procedures".

This handbook was a priceless resource for Sarah and many others who had to adhere to Nevada's notarial regulations or wished to become notaries. Everything was covered, including the requirements for getting a commission and detailed instructions for performing various notarial acts.

In plain language, "Unlocking the Public Realm" provided easily understood explanations of Nevada's notarial procedures. Whatever their degree of experience, anyone considering becoming a notary should definitely check out this comprehensive guide.As Sarah found out, one needs to be fully conversant with notarial procedures in order to execute financial and legal documents in Nevada.

A Notary Public

A person with a track record of honesty who serves as an unbiased witness for the signing of important papers, such as powers of attorney, wills, trusts, statements, and court depositions, is known as a notary public, or simply a notary. Notaries are chosen by state governments as public workers, putting them in a position of power and responsibility.

What Does Getting a Document Notarized Mean?

Three components make up notarizations, also known as notarial actions:

- To ensure that the paper is valid, the notary signs and stamps it.
- The act is written by the notary public in a notary notebook.preserving
- The notary confirms the signer's name, desire to sign, and understanding of the details of the paper.

The Advantages of Document Notarization

This method has lasted for millennia for the following reasons:

- **Prevent the need for a witness to come into court**: A signed paper is considered self-authenticating under the law of proof. This means that it may be used as proof in court without further confirmation that it is who it claims to be. Consequently, a notarization saves a great deal of time and money by eliminating the requirement for the witness to be present.
- **Boost the document's credibility**: Many papers lack legal power unless they have been signed. A notarization is helpful even if this doesn't apply to all papers since the notary's seal and

signature improve the document's innate value and validity.

- **Offer legal defense**: Getting your papers signed might help you stay clear of lawsuits and contract disagreements.
- **Prevent fraud:** Having a reliable agent confirm a signer's name adds an extra layer of security while completing important papers in a world where con artists prey on any unknown person.

Becoming a Notary Public in Nevada

- Eligibility Requirements

- Application Process

- Commissioning

In Nevada, anyone who is interested in a career path that is both professional and helpful may become a notary public. Notaries are qualified to perform related tasks such as administering oaths and signing legal papers.

The process for becoming a notary public are:

- Purchase a four-year, $10,000 security bond.
- Receive a filing notice from the county clerk's office after the submission of your notary bond and the administration of the oath of office.

You will need the filing letter in order to complete the application on the secretary of state's website.

- Go to the website of the State of Nevada Notary Public Training, create an account, and finish the Notary Public Training Course by following the instructions in the course catalog. then succeed in the Notary Public Commission Exam, which is given by the Secretary of State's Notary Division. The training and test must be completed in order to submit your notary application.
- Create an account on the Nevada Business Portal, fill out the notary public application, and print it off. The notary's selection option is "Appointment for Application and Training Fee."
- Print out the notary application that is already filled out and sign it in blue ink. Electronic-signature applications will not be accepted,

- Submit your application online once you have logged into your Nevada Business Portal account.

  To apply, the candidate for notary must perform the following:

- Please find included your signed notary public application.
- Please provide the filing notice that you were sent by the county clerk.
- Please provide the notary training certificate.
- Pay the $35 application fee and $45 notary training costs to become a notary.
- Obtain a notary stamp after the secretary of state's approval.

Qualification requirements:

To become a notary in Nevada, you must meet the requirements listed below:

- Have grown to be eighteen years old.
- Be a resident of Nevada or a nearby state who keeps a place of employment or resides there on a regular basis.
- If you have ever been convicted of a crime involving moral turpitude, you may request the restoration of your civil rights.

Commission process:

1. Upon receipt, the Secretary of State's office will check the completed application for correctness and completeness.

2. If accepted, the Secretary of State's office will issue a four-year Notary Public license.
3. The person will get a commission certificate and a notarial seal.
4. The person has to swear an oath of office in front of a clerk, attorney, or other authorized official.
5. In accordance with the state's notarial rules and regulations, the notary public must keep a log of every notarial act they conduct.

The only options to become a notary public in Nevada are to fulfil the qualifications, pass the licensing test, and complete the application process.

Steps involved in obtaining an electronic notary commission in Nevada

Naturally, of course! Getting an electronic notary commission in Nevada involves a number of specific steps and requirements that ensure notaries are ready to perform electronic notarizations in compliance with state laws and regulations. The necessary actions to become an electronic notary public in Nevada are as follows:

1. Meet Eligibility Requirements: Applicants must first meet the requirements listed by the Nevada Secretary of State's office in order to be eligible for an electronic notary commission in Nevada. Prerequisites for eligibility typically include having a current Nevada notary public commission and meeting any additional requirements specific to appointments as an electronic notary, like finishing training in electronic notarization protocols.

2. Completion of Electronic Notary Training: A specialized education in the methods and processes of electronic notarization is required of aspiring electronic notaries in Nevada. Among the unique aspects of electronic notarization that are covered in this training are the use of electronic signatures and seals, identity verification, and electronic notary hardware and software. In order to ensure that electronic notaries are aware of the standards and best practices for carrying out electronic notarial acts, approved providers may provide training courses.

3. Obtain an Electronic Notary Bond and Insurance: In order to apply for an Electronic Notary Commission, you must first obtain an Electronic Notary Bond and, in some cases, Electronic Notary Errors and

Omissions Insurance. The electronic notary bond provides financial protection for the public in the event that the electronic notary makes mistakes or behaves improperly. Professional liability coverage is also provided by errors and omissions insurance to further safeguard electronic notaries for their notarial work.

4. Submit Application to the Secretary of State: After meeting the prerequisites listed above, applicants for an electronic notary commission are required to submit an application to the Nevada Secretary of State's office. The application usually requires obtaining the electronic notary bond, providing documentation that the electronic notary training was completed, and fulfilling any additional administrative requirements that the Secretary of State may specify.

5. Approval and Issuance of Electronic Notary Commission: Following receipt and review of the application, the Nevada Secretary of State's office will assess the applicant's qualifications and compliance with the requirements for an electronic notary commission. If the application is approved, the candidate will receive an electronic notary commission that will allow them to electronically notarize documents in accordance with Nevada law.

6. Obtain Approved Electronic Notary Software and Hardware: Following the issuance of their electronic notary commission, Nevada regulations require electronic notaries to adhere to technological and security standards for the software and hardware they use. This may apply to the purchase of electronic signature solutions, secure electronic seal devices, digital certificate technology, and other necessary equipment for electronic notarizations.

7. Maintain Compliance and Renewal: It is the responsibility of Nevada's electronic notaries to ensure that they stay in compliance with all applicable laws and regulations regarding electronic notarization. This means ensuring the security of electronic notarization processes, maintaining compliance with state-mandated recordkeeping and retention requirements, and renewing the electronic notary commission.

People must follow the guidelines and fulfil the requirements in order to become an electronic notary commission holder in Nevada and perform electronic notarizations in a manner compliant with the legal and technological framework governing electronic notarial acts.

Process of electronic notarization in Nevada

Electronic notarization in Nevada involves the use of electronic signatures and seals to notarize documents, enhancing the convenience and efficiency of the notarial process. The process of electronic notarization in Nevada follows a set of specific procedures and requirements to ensure the validity and security of electronically notarized documents.

Here are the key components of the electronic notarization process in Nevada:

1. Electronic Notary Commission: In Nevada, notaries who wish to perform electronic notarizations must obtain a specific electronic notary commission. This commission authorizes the notary to conduct electronic notarizations in compliance with state regulations. Notaries must meet additional qualifications and undergo training to obtain this specialized commission.

2. Electronic Notary Software and Hardware: Electronic notaries are required to use approved electronic notary software and hardware that comply with Nevada's electronic notarization laws and regulations. This may include specific electronic signature solutions, digital certificate technology, and secure electronic seal devices. The software and hardware must meet stringent security and authentication standards to ensure the integrity of electronic notarizations.

3. Authentication and Identity Verification: Prior to performing an electronic notarization, the electronic notary must verify the identity of the individual seeking the notarization. This typically involves using electronic identity verification methods, such as knowledge-based authentication questions or biometric verification. The notary must confirm the identity of the signer using approved electronic identification credentials.

4. Electronic Notarization Process: When conducting an electronic notarization, the electronic notary applies their electronic signature and electronic seal to the document using the approved electronic notary software and hardware. The electronic signature and seal serve as the notarial act, indicating the notary's official endorsement of the document. The electronic notarization process may involve additional electronic records to capture the notarial act and related information.

5. Electronic Notarization Certificate: An electronic notarization certificate is created and appended to the electronically notarized document upon the electronic notary's completion of the electronic notarization process. The date and time of the notarial act, the notary's electronic signature and seal, and other relevant information mandated by Nevada law are all contained in the electronic notarization certificate.

6. Maintenance and Retention of Electronic Records: Nevada-based electronic notaries are accountable for the safekeeping of electronic records related to the notarial acts they carry out, including certificates of electronic notarization and related electronic documents. To maintain their accessibility and integrity, electronic notarial records must comply with certain recordkeeping regulations for the duration of the legally required retention period.

7. Rules and Regulations Compliance: Nevada law establishes requirements for electronic notarization, which electronic notaries must follow. These requirements include any security and technological requirements specific to electronic notarial acts. For electronically notarized documents to be legally valid and admissible in Nevada courts and other official proceedings, adherence to these standards is necessary.

Electronic notaries can execute notarial acts with the same legal force as conventional paper-based notarizations by according to these guidelines and the regulatory framework governing electronic notarization in Nevada. This accelerated notarization procedure improves efficiency, security, accessibility, and the authenticity and integrity of the notarial process by utilizing electronic technologies.

Overview of Notarial Acts in Nevada

- Jurisdiction and Powers of a Notary

There are legal steps that a notary public must take to make sure that documents are signed correctly, that someone is telling the truth, or that certain events are witnessed. These steps are called "notarial acts." Notaries public in Nevada are allowed to do different notarial tasks as long as they follow certain rules and limitations.

In Nevada, a notary can take acknowledgments, administer oaths or affirmations, witness signatures, make certified copies, check vehicle identification numbers (VINs), and perform marriage ceremonies. Each of these acts has specific requirements that must be fulfilled before a notary public can perform them.

One thing that Nevada notaries public can do is administer oaths and affirmations. In other words, they can be a legal witness when someone signs an affidavit or other legal document and can give the person signing the document an oath or affirmation to make them swear that the information in the document is true.

It's also necessary for a Nevada notary public to have the right to do a notarial act. This means that the notary's power is mostly limited to the state of Nevada. They can't do notarial work outside of Nevada unless they have special permission to do so.

However, a Nevada notary public can refuse to perform a notarial act if they have reason to believe that the document is fake or that the signatory is not authorized to sign the document. They can also ask to see and look over identification documents.

A Nevada notary public is an important part of the legal system because they are an impartial third party who witnesses the signing of papers and other legal events. Notaries public have certain duties and powers that are meant to make sure they do their jobs honestly and professionally.

Notarial Certificate

- Types of Notarial Certificates
- Proper Execution of Notarial Certificates

Notarial papers are legal statements that the public signs, dates, and swears to. They check the signer's name, attest to their free writing, and witness to the notary public's appearance at the document's signing. A notarial certificate is a necessary component of many legal papers, such as powers of attorney, deeds, trusts, and wills.

Notarial Certificate Types:

- **Acknowledgment Certificate:** When a signer certifies that they have signed a document willingly, they use this kind of notarial certificate. A power of attorney, mortgage, and property are among the legal papers for which an acceptance letter is often needed.

- **Jurat Certificate**: This kind of certificate is used for signing papers that call for an oath or statement to be made. A jurat certificate is often used in court papers such as statements and depositions.

- **Certified Copy Certificate**: When a notary public makes a certified copy of an original document, they use this kind of notarial certificate. For birth certificates, marriage certificates, and other government papers, a verified copy certificate is often used

Correct Notarial Certificate Execution:

1. **Confirm the signer's identity:** The notary public must confirm the signer's

identity by studying a government-issued identification document that includes a physical description, signature, and picture.

2. **Fill out the notarial certificate**: The notary public is needed to fill out the notarial certificate with all important information, such as the date, kind of certificate, and other details.

3. **Sign the notarial certificate**: The notary public must sign the paper using their full name, not the one they use on a daily basis, as it shows on their commission.

4. **Apply the notary seal**: The certificate, which includes the notary's commission information, seal type, and end date, has to have the notary seal put on it.

5. **Maintain a notarial record:** The notary is required to put the notarial act into their official notarial notebook, where they must record the signer's information, the type of paper, and the notarial certificate that was finished.Notaries may check the accuracy of legal papers and properly perform a notarial certificate by sticking to these processes.

Record-keeping and Journal Entry

- Importance of Record-keeping

- Journal Entry Requirements and Best Practices

- Retention and Storage of Notarial Records

Keeping records and journal entries are significant pieces of your day to day obligations as a notary public .A notary's journal is a composed record of each notarial act the legal official finishes, complete with marks, dates, times, and other relevant data.

The significance of keeping up with record-keeping couldn't possibly be more significant. record-keeping gives a dependable, durable record of the notarial act finished. They act as proof in legal disputes also. Keeping a journal guarantees the honesty of the notarial interaction and is fundamental for forestalling extortion.

Journal entries are administered by state regulations, and notaries are expected to follow industry best practices and explicit rules. At a minimum, journal entries should include the following: the date, the time, the type of notarial act performed, the name and signature of the document, and the kind of recognizable proof introduced ought to be in every way remembered for journal entries, in any event. It's likewise encouraged to take note of the kind and date of the record being legally approved.

The journal should be kept up with in a precise, exact, and lucid way. It is fitting to forgo remembering superfluous subtleties as this might create turmoil for what's in store. All sections should be written in ink on the grounds that eliminating or changing any of them could think twice about respectability of the notarial act.

Notarial records should be kept and put away as per state regulation. They ought to be kept in a completely safe spot to forestall harm, robbery, and unapproved access. In specific states, public accountants are expected to keep up with their Journals on record for a particular time frame. After the maintenance period has slipped by, it is urgent to fittingly discard the records.

All in all, keeping journal entries and record keeping is a fundamental piece of the notarial cycle. They act as proof of the notarial act executed, safeguard the underwriter's advantages, and keep up with the honesty of the notarial cycle.Notaries should comply with state regulations and best practices to guarantee that their records are exact, finished, and safely put away

Identification and confirmation

-Acceptable Forms of Identification

- Verification Procedures

Acceptable Forms of Identification:

Notaries in Nevada are required to check one or more government-issued forms of identification, such as a driver's license or passport, in order to confirm the name of the person writing the paper.

Verification Methods:

Notaries in Nevada are allowed to use any of two methods for confirming an identity:

(1) personal information or

(2) acceptable proof.

Personal knowledge denotes that the notary is already acquainted with the witness and knows who they are. In order to provide acceptable proof, one or more pieces of identification that meet the notary's verification standards must be provided. Notaries need to be certain that the name being offered is real, appropriately safe, and pertains to the person giving it. The sort of identification that is given must also be mentioned by the notary in their diary. A notary may sometimes additionally need further documents or proof of identity, such as biometric information or questions requiring specialized knowledge.

Preventing Fraud

- Recognizing Fraudulent Activities

- Steps to Prevent Notarial Fraud

It is very important for notaries public to be able to spot fraud. Notarial fraud can have very bad legal and financial effects on everyone involved. Finding fraudulent activity is the first step in stopping notarial fraud. You can spot fraud with the help of the following tips:

- Look for signs that the document has been changed, like correction fluid, erasures, and changes in the colour or handwriting of the ink.

- Being careful when notarizing papers from family, close friends, or anyone else you have a personal or financial connection with is important.

- Be careful reading documents that are missing important information or have blank spaces.

- Be aware of any signs of pressure or coercion, like someone trying to rush you through the process or insisting on a notarization outside of normal business hours or somewhere you don't normally go.

Along with recognizing notarial fraud when it happens, it is important to do something to stop it. The following advice can help avoid notarial fraud:

- Verify the signer's identity by looking through official identification documents and confirming the details they provided about themselves.

- Keep a thorough record of all the details in your notary journal, such as the type of document notarized, the date and time of the notarization, and the full names and identifying information of the signers.

Inform the public about the value of notary services and the notary public's responsibility to uphold the integrity of the notarial profession.

- Keep yourself informed about the most recent notary laws and regulations to make sure you are acting appropriately and morally.

These guidelines for identifying and stopping notarial fraud will help you protect your clients and yourself from the dangers and repercussions of dishonest behaviour.

Fees and Charges

- Fee Regulations for Notarial Services
- Prohibited Fee Practices

Fee Regulations for Notarial Services:

It is mandatory for Notaries Public in every state to follow the fee guidelines established by the state administration. These charges are typically calculated as a fixed sum for each notarial act or signature.

Prohibited Payment Methods:

It is also important for Notaries Public to be aware of fee practices that are forbidden and may result in fines or other legal repercussions. Charging for services that were not rendered, charging exorbitant fees, and charging various rates to different clients are a few instances of forbidden fee practices. It's also crucial to remember that notaries are not eligible to receive tips or gratuities for their services.

Ethics and Professional Responsibility

- Code of Professional Responsibility for Notaries Public

- Consequences of Violating Ethical

In order to maintain the integrity of the notarial process and shield the public from potential fraud or misrepresentation, notaries public are required to uphold the highest ethical and professional standards. Understanding the Code of Professional Responsibility for Notaries Public, which outlines the moral standards that all notaries must uphold, is the first step toward accomplishing this goal.

Fairness, impartiality, and honesty are encouraged in the notarial profession through a number of significant provisions found in the Code of Professional Responsibility for Notaries Public. Notaries must, for instance, ensure that signers are who they say they are, keep correct notarial records, and prominently display their commission. Additionally, they are not allowed to behave in any way that might be interpreted as undermining their objectivity or posing a conflict of interest. If a notary public transgresses the Code of Professional Responsibility, there will be dire repercussions. A notary may lose their commission permanently and be subject to civil or criminal penalties if they violate ethical standards. In certain cases, notaries public may even be held personally accountable for losses brought on by their unethical behaviour. Notaries must be conscious of the possible repercussions of acting unethically and take action to guarantee that they are always conducting themselves with the utmost professionalism and integrity. This could entail going to training sessions, asking professional associations for advice, and talking to colleagues or legal counsel about moral conundrums. Ultimately, in order to gain the public's trust and respect and make a substantial contribution to the accurate execution and recording of significant legal and financial documents, notaries must uphold the highest ethical and professional standards. Notaries can preserve the integrity of the notarial profession while upholding the highest standards of professionalism and ethics by adhering to the Code of Professional Responsibility.

Guidelines for Professional Conduct

It is necessary for notaries to maintain high moral and expert standards in order to protect the general welfare. Notaries must stick to strict rules in the performance of their tasks and must act impartially and with secrecy. Guidelines for professional behaviour help notaries know how to stick to these rules.

Professionalism: It is expected of notaries to always act in a professional manner. This involves being on time, thoughtful, and kind to customers.

Confidentiality: Notaries are expected to keep any information they handle during notarial acts absolutely hidden. They must not provide any illegal parties access to any business information.

Continuing Education: It is important for notaries to be updated about changes to the laws and rules relating to their job. The information and skills of notaries may be better with further study.

Renewal, revocation, and suspension of commission

Renewal, revocation, and suspension of commission are important aspects of notary publics in Nevada.

Renewal Process and Requirements:

Nevada notary commissions are valid for four years. Notaries must send a completed application and payment to the Secretary of State's office in order to renew their commission. A six-hour notary education course must also be finished by notaries before they can renew their commission. Topics including notary laws, best practices, and ethical considerations are covered in the education course.

Grounds for Revocation or Suspension of Commission:

If a notary violates any notary laws or regulations, their commission may be revoked or suspended. A commission may be revoked or suspended for a number of reasons, such as: fraudulent or dishonest behaviour while carrying out notarial duties; improper journal maintenance; incapacity or unfitness to perform notarial acts; felony conviction; and misuse of the notarial seal

Appeals Process:

A notary may file an appeal in the event that their commission is revoked or suspended.

The notice of revocation or suspension must be received, and the appeal must be filed, within fifteen days. The Secretary of State's office hears the appeal, and the notary has the right to legal representation during that process. The notary may petition the district court for judicial review if their appeal is rejected.

In order to maintain their good standing, Nevada notaries are required to adhere to specific rules and regulations. In addition to abstaining from breaking notary laws and regulations and filing an appeal if their commission is in danger of being suspended or revoked, they also have to renew their commission every four years.

Frequently Asked Questions

- Common Questions and Answers about Notarial Procedures in Nevada

Yes, the following are some typical Q&As regarding Nevadan notarial procedures along with their responses:

What does a notary public do and what is the role of one?
A notary public is a person designated by the state government to serve as an unbiased, neutral witness during the signing of significant documents. Notaries make an official record of the transaction, confirm the signers' identities, and make sure they are signing voluntarily and knowing what is contained in the document.

Does getting something notarized require an appointment?

No, appointments are not necessary in order to notarize a document. To make sure the notary is available and that they can notarize the kind of document you require, it is a good idea to give them a call in advance.

What is the fee to have something notarized in Nevada?
A notary public in Nevada is permitted to charge $5 for each signature. The most a notary can charge per signature is $5, however some notaries may charge a flat rate for their services.

Is it possible for a notary to notarize a non-English document?
A notary public in Nevada is not permitted to notarize documents that are not in English unless they are proficient in the language and have a thorough understanding of the document's contents.

How can I obtain an apostille and what does it entail?
A document's official certification of authenticity that is accepted in other

countries is known as an apostille. In Nevada, the original document needs to be submitted to the Secretary of State's office along with a request form and payment in order to receive an apostille.

Is a notary able to provide legal advice?

No, notaries public are not permitted to draft legal documents or offer legal advice in Nevada. All they can do is watch as documents are signed and confirm the signers' identities.

What is the duration of a notary public's commission in Nevada?

In Nevada, notary commissions are valid for four years. Notaries must renew their commission every four years in order to keep serving as notaries public.

Glossary

- Commonly Used Terms and Definitions in Notarial Procedures

Yes, here is a potential glossary of terms and definitions used frequently in notarial procedures:

The notarial act known as an **acknowledgment** is when a notary public confirms a signer's identity and attests to the signer's voluntary and understanding signature on a document.

Affirmation: A statement under penalty of perjury that a signer makes regarding the veracity and accuracy of the information in a document.

Attestation is the process of seeing a notary public sign a document.

Certification is a notarial act wherein a public notary attests to the accuracy and truthfulness of a document copy.

A notary public administers an oath or affirmation to a document signer, asking them to attest to the truth and accuracy of the document's contents. This notarial act is known as a jurat.

A public official designated by law as a notary public is able to administer oaths and affirmations, certify documents, and carry out other notarial functions.

An oath is a formal promise made by the signatory to a document that the information is true and accurate; noncompliance bears the penalty of perjury.

A protest is a notarial act in which a public notary attests to the refusal to accept or pay a promissory note or bill of exchange.

A notary public will use a seal, which is an official mark or impression, to verify that a document has been notarized.

A person who signs a document in front of a notary public is known as the **signer**.

Verification is the act of a notary public attesting to the authenticity of a document, the identity of the signer, and the fact that the signer signed the document willingly and understandingly.

Conclusion

Best Practices for Nevada Notaries are :Keeping a professional manner, confirming signers' names, keeping accurate records, avoiding conflicts of interest, and abstaining from false activity are some suggested best practices for Nevada notaries. It could be necessary for notaries to join training classes in order to improve their skills and stay current on laws, rules, and moral principles.

Resources for Ongoing Education: Notaries may acquire more knowledge and experience in carrying out their duties by participating in continuing education classes and using online tools. Access to exact information on legal requirements, possible social problems, and strategies to stop scams in notarial deals are some examples of these tools.